LADY DEATH

and other poems
venerating change

KEATH SILVA

ISBN 978-1-66782-064-4

LADY DEATH

DEDICATION

I dedicate this book to all the
trans, non-binary and gender non-conforming people,
those who came before,
those now living and those yet to come.

APPRECIATION

I offer my gratitude to my two children
Theresa and Matoska
who teach me about birth, love and letting go.

Many thanks to
Dylan Wilder Quinn,
Alok Vaid-Menon,
Mars Wright and Max Pearl
for your transgender and gender non-confirming
inspirational empowerment!

CONTENTS

FOREWORD

The poems of *Lady Death* are, to me, travel writing. They suggest a voyage. I read them as trails marked in wood and in breadcrumbs through uncharted territory; as prayers and letters from long ocean journeys, topographical sketches of the terrible and transformative terrain of grief, tender whisperings and tears shed in hollow night shelters of earth and stone, chthonic and animal and botanical love songs, epistles from home. What do we do with these multiform maps? They are not the kind we are meant to follow. They are the kind meant to tell a story, to inspire and offer hope and courage. Keath's poems are travel writing. They suggest a voyage. They speak to us of the myriad adventures and paths home that await each of us, fellow travelers, in *terra incognita*.

Meenakshi Poolapalli

"Trans Joy is Resistance."
Mars Wright

PROEM

This collection of poems is a companion for you as you walk through the seasons of change in your life.

These poems are the sweat of my gender transition, the tears of my trauma, the kernels of the reclamation of authentic self and the fruit stones of much tasting, chewing and elicitation.

These renderings are born from the process of biting into harsh realities, tasting them and rolling them around my mouth, until they become smooth and palpable, exposing their many sides and nuances, so that their medicine can be extracted for nourishment and growth. These poems are drenched in support from the healing power of nature, who is the ultimate teacher on embracing death and dying to make way for living life to its fullest.

What you are about to experience is the veneration of the process of meeting one's own pain and tender vulnerability. It is in this encounter that oppressive structures, worn out coping strategies and opaque distracting clutter pass away, giving rise to a surprising and refreshing down-to-the-bone self-intimacy and realness.

My hope is that this book will support you in being gentle with yourself as you experience, loss, change and deepening in authenticity.

LADY DEATH

Being Trans Is Beautiful

Being trans is beautiful

We walk between the worlds
We see from all sides
We have faced oppression
and have found freedom
or death

We break barriers
We build bridges
We open the possibility
of authenticity for everyone

Thank You My Allies

When you call me by the name and pronouns I adore,
you give me
a gentle warm hug
a hand up
a healing balm
a bright smile in the dark
a heart opening wink
a bouquet of Sunflowers
a Yarrow blossom circle of protection
a tender Rose of sweetness
years on my life
a burst of energy
the ability to focus
a nourishing sense of safety and belonging
a happy memory
a warm cup of Lemon Balm love

When you call me by the name and pronouns I adore,
you give me
wellness, welcome and home

Thank You

At the Center of Things

Find your ground in me
in the smooth white bone
at the center of things

There are wrinkles in the fabric
you lay down before me
stretch them taut
in their glistening blue hues
and adorn me my beloved
wrap me in this cloak of night sky
and bring Roses to my mouth
for when you fall in love
with that which you most fear
the ride
though raucous and mysterious
becomes drenched in starlight
and the bony hand
warm behind your heart
nudges you forward
to abounding joy

Misgendered

I liken how I feel when you call me lady or ma'am
to being a balloon that has been suddenly popped,
an unexpected slap in the face
a jolt, a fright
a startling concern that maybe
we are living in different universes
and therefore I am utterly alone,
invisible and lost to the day

I feel angry when I am misgendered
my heart races
because I have been
branded
stamped
labelled
boxed
denied access
to truth and connection
completely misunderstood
not accounted for, un-protected, not remembered

Being misgendered
derails my day
like a train knocked off its track
a child falling off a swing
or a bird being shot in mid-flight

I try to shield myself
from being misgendered
by staying home
not going to parties
declining social invitations
lowering my voice

wearing certain clothing
avoiding certain people, circles, towns, establishments
procrastinating on phone calls
walking with a strut
wearing a pronoun mask, hat, shirt, button
and, still, the onslaught continues

Each time it happens,
the quandary faces me
Shall I defend and assert myself
thus enduring the excuses, the hostility,
the falling all over themselves with guilt,
the explanations, the defenses
the cascade of them hating themselves
because I exist?
Or shall I just take the blow, shrink,
grab my groceries and go?

Allowing *Lady Death* into my life
is the freedom
of allowing the word "lady"
and all the torture wrapped up in it
to die
making space
for the sound of
who *I am*
to fly

The River of Your Crying

Of course
you long
to curl into yourself
and find comfort

We all do

There are pathways
to this relief
this cessation of
the unabating
pulse of irritation
the dull roar of apprehension
the constant ache of disappointment
the ceaseless fear of not measuring up
not fitting in
the terror of being cast out

Some roads lead to a temporary numb
that robs you of your dignity
some avenues take you to a thrill
that blots out
the rumble of agony
that haunts you

Some boulevards empty
into chaos
that pulls you away
from the tortuous inner moment at hand
long enough to relieve its pressure
for an hour, a day, a week, a year, a decade
when it returns pushing you down
yet another street of escape

And then there are those walkways
though arduous to find
that lead you to the helpers
And in that vulnerable pause
when you touch your own torment
with one warm curious hand
and you reach the other hand
out
trembling
however tenuously
it is met
with the warm reaching fingers
of surrender and grace
community clouds and Moss
and you are pulled to a place
that once beholden
removes the longing
for the other circles of despair
that only prolong this reckoning

Softly curl now
into the quiet earth
with a bouquet of Yarrow
Rose and Rue
clutched to your heart
whose song now fills you
and lets loose
the river of your crying

Lady Death

Lady Death
you are not too shy
to reach
through
the flesh of my back
to take hold
of my spine
to shake out the chunks
of frozen ash
squeeze out
the pools of pus
and kill
the infections invaders
that rob me of my light

Oh, how I adore you Lady Death
for capturing the intruders
that caged me with their lies
and sending them forth
to source themselves
elsewhere—away from here

Oh, how I adore you Lady Death
for it is your song that initiates
the draining
of swollen comfort
revealing the eager and able
task within

Oh, how I adore you Lady Death
for wringing out
the paste they fed me
to assuage their inability
to feel the pain
passed down to them
bone to bone

year after year
hidden in the opaque
color of mucus
in the untreated wounds
of blood and family lines

Oh, how I adore you Lady Death
for circling and lighting up
with your bony finger
the charred-flesh scar
in my brain
caused by the burning
brand of abuse
and shock
for calling your *colibrí*
to draw nectar
from the eye
of the twisted lesion
opening pathways
to reignite
flash and pulse

We are moving
We are here
We are feeling
and alive

And with your reign of compassion
you place this island
of awakening ancient dormancy
in my palm
I delight in the rootlets
fondling their way
through forgotten shadows
and return this spiraling blossom
into my own brain
to hear a cacophony of

Welcome home! and
This is where we live!

And oh, the depth of this medicine
the hummingbird brings forth
from the breaking of our hearts!

Oh, Lady Death, shake me all you want
for there is no solace left for me
in this puffiness, this creaking sofa, this hiding

And the striking sound
of the curtains falling away
the clanking of your ribs as you dance
and the burst of emotion
exploding in my chest
is the bread, butter and honey
I have been starving for

Ultimate Spoon

Wrap me in bones
this morning
the ultimate spoon
your breath
ancient sand
so course
and honeyed
sends me
further
into the marrow
of who I was
when small
There is solace
in getting
to the bottom of things
sending resonance
to the inside
of my own spine
touching into places
that had become
foggy and opaque
unreachable

Hold me here
where there is no running
and the hidden places melt and open
in your inmost glow
radiating its warmth
like being found
like familiar eyes looking
at the scars
letting loose salty tears
of hearts connecting
after such a long
and lonely dark

Stay
so I don't go back
to shattered

Be with me
so I don't go back
to scattered

Help me untangle
each ulna, femur, patella
laying them together
reassembled
whole, home
and breathing
in the quiet
of the morning
autumn light

Relentless Summer

Where is sanctuary
from the fire and smoke
from your soft cheek resting on the curb
inches away from endless cars racing by
those pleading eyes begging for help
the masks, the fear
the distance

Where is sanctuary
from the blaring lights
the family patterns repeating
people clinging to the plane
as it flies away
dropping them
to their death
The searing pain
of the lonely rooms of childhood
rising each time something reminds us

Where is sanctuary
from the challenge
the test
the responsibility
the burden

Endless acres of
dead orchards
and
burnt forest
veteran tent homes
lining the streets
in Brentwood

Where is sanctuary
from changing lanes
avoiding rush hour
the constant chime of phones
the incessant dance of neon
and streetlights' repetitive cycle
of yellow, green, red
The helpless agony of watching
the ones I love ache and bleed
with life's ceaseless blows

Where is the dark
small hole
so quiet
where the cool earth pulls out
the frenzied chaos from my skin
as I trace the smooth red
curling roots
with my fingers
inhaling soil and leaves
rocks between my toes
the sound of water

I see this doorway
this possibility
this seed of serenity
in every
Jacaranda blossom
each vibrant mural
cascading over brick and stone
I hear it in the children's laughter
as they run down
a thin sliver of grass

Let me nuzzle tonight
into your giant furry body
like a small, small creature
who lost their way
then you gave them shelter

Stroke my head
as you coo
painting spirals of mud
on my weary forehead

Let me rest here a while
while you watch over the world
and this heavy-handed
summer full moon
begins to wane

Autumn Full Moon

Pressing at the back of my heart
smack between these wet fledgling wings
an invisible unyielding hand
supports yet breaks open
my trembling adoration
for the sanctuary of decomposition
the shelter of endings
the shrine of death

For the sweet scent of decay
after the long snowy winter of silence
sets free the new baby seeds
bursting forth so tender
through fallen leaves and duff
reaching for the warm
rays of sunlight
on the morn after the wind stills
and the pelting rain has quieted

My heart feels stitchy and stretchy
as it yawns and swells
with an agitated wonder
A thousand elbows nudging
at the inside wall of this confining cavern
A grunting dampened rage
pushing its way out of tightened mouths
A groan that crescendos into a wail
and curls the spine
like a fiddlehead
milking out resistance and refusal,
that holds it down, down
beneath remembering

Dance, play and rest
feed the poetic soul
and when wild feline tooth and jaw
are hungry for
the strangled wads of flesh
stagnating in your belly
concealing the putrid lies
and dreadful fears of
"It is selfish to create."
"Art is a waste of time."
"No-one wants what you are making."

Let Her feast while snarling
and replenish
the freedom in Her step
the sharp in Her claws
the gleam in Her eyes

As She dances through
the green jungle
of density and matter and lust

Cry here with me
as the misty moon rises
over the damp field of Dogwood and Plum
bowing to the ground
in the balm of release
the cascade of tears

Returning
to the imperceivable eye gaze
of presence and spine-tickling delight
as summer slips through our fingers
and the Autumn full moon brings the rains

Let Fall to the Ground

My heart feels the way a wound does
as it begins to heal
kind of itchy around the edges
with a buzz of new pink skin
growing to close the gaps

My heart feels like the morning after a fever has broken
when you know the worst is over
but you are still weakened from the heat
and there is a quiet Hallelujah!
to find yourself still alive
and hopeful in this new dawn

My heart feels like a garden
that was just run over by a tractor
but a few hours have passed
and some of the trampled plants begin
to lift themselves out of the mud
and reach once again towards the sun

My heart feels like a wet hacky sack
sitting alone in the grass
after being kicked around a circle of eager feet and knees
butts and backs the satisfying smack
of human contact so fleeting
like a dance made of shadows
just resting now in the sunsetting ache

My heart feels like a horse
that has been rode hard and put away wet
and although the stench, dust and throb
are piercing and dull
there is relief in knowing the rider is off my back
and there are no more miles to walk tonight
while the stars are shining

My heart feels like a Pomegranate
that life cherished for a while
sinking its shining teeth into the leathery flesh
to suck the red juices and let fall to the ground,
whose kernels are just beginning
to soften, break and sprout
as I tentatively reach my fledging supple roots
into
new
welcoming
ground

A Message from Below 1

I feast on your pain
thereby relieving you
of your burden

I absorb
what you
need
to forget

To me
death is
so sweet

The musky odor
of rotting
is my perfume

Release
your cares
and finished things
to me

Revel
in the moments
between

That fallow
place
of
possibility

Don't shy
away

From
watching things
fall
away

It is in this
departure
that
you
taste
your
soul

A Message from Below 2

I feast on your fear
that electric
delicacy
of your
desire
to
go
on
in warmth
and wellness
unmolested
so your dreams
surface
and
your breathing
softens

Your drive
to preserve
your okay-ness
as manifesting
in your terror
is succulent
for me

Offer me
your fear
with Basil
and tear drops
Oh, aromatic sauce

Your sweaty palms
and racing heart
allow me
to taste them
and devour them
between
my ancient
teeth

I open for you
the nectar
of forever
and
serve
you
your
eternity

Pride

I pushed down my inner sense of who I was
and lived deeply there
away from all of you
I used to wrestle with the boys
I was one of them
with my king snake
wrapped around my neck
gripping the handlebars
of my dirt bike
tick-tocking
on my skateboard
until a familiar
friendly boy-punch at play
made my chest
strangely hurt
and a little bump grew
where his fist had landed

I said, "Hey! Look what you did to me!"
But it kept on growing,
and then the other breast bud
joined in this unexpected betrayal

I tried to wash-off
those *trespassing* lumps
with 1,000 tears in the shower
But they swelled into something
the boys blushed over,
giggled and grabbed at,
and because of their pointed presence,
I was treated in a whole new way

Not sensing any footing,
no semblance of agency

as who I *knew* myself to be
slipped through my fingers like water
I took hold of a poisonous power
offered to me on the daily
"I see you took your pretty pills today."
"I am going to want your number in a few years."

I wielded that pretty girl power
even as I detested it
to prove that I was something
you wanted
someone of any value
who might not be killed
for another day
who might have the chance
of being kept

I wielded that pretty girl power
to twist you into knots
to have a false strength of influence
on a sinking ship
to break your heart
like the pain
of those teasing words
that ripped me apart

Dressed in white gloves
and patent leather shoes
I scowled
My very life seemed threatened
by the impossibility
of me getting to wear a tux
and to be the one to say
"May I have this dance?"

I didn't have words
for the chasm widening
between my inner world
and the mask of survival
I donned

When the teacher said,
"Girls on one side, boys on the other,"
my inner voice asked,
"Where then shall I go?"

When I was seen kissing Jennifer
in front of my grey locker
a circle of jeerers
threw dagger words
which ripped
to shreds
the awakening glimmer of my true essence
which I had just tasted on her lips

"You dirty Lesbian."
"You are disgusting."
"You have the grossest cooties."
"You stay away from us!"

A part of me died that day
as I blotted out
my own fledgling spark
and started getting high
very high
and often
And giving my body
that had already betrayed me
away
to boys
and men
for their pleasure

for the fleeting hope
that I would pass for "normal"
that I would not be utterly
cast out of all
warmth of humanity
just for being who I am
and loving who I love

This thing of who we are
who we know ourselves to be
on the inside
cannot actually be driven
out of us

Each time
I got close
to living the truth
of who I am
something came to strike me down
triggering the memory
of the teenagers
throwing
blade slurs
at me
by the lockers
And I would push it
all back down
and hard

This thing of who we are
who we know ourselves to be
on the inside
cannot actually be driven
out of us

And one day
the closet has no door
so you burn down
the whole house
and you don't give a fuck
what people think

But truthfully you do
and it hurts every day
to be told that
who you are
is not ok

But you are out
and you live any way
and you find people like you
reaching out their hands
and their hearts

This skyscraper pile
of shove after shove
has taken me years
to uncover

And every pain-in-the-ass
obstacle to tackle
every hurdle
every insult
every threat
every fear
has all been worth it
to live myself
as I know myself to be
on the inside

Sprout

There is a pain
lurking
in the folds
of forgotten shirts and dresses
bunched behind boxes
in the very back of your closet
pushed aside
for even a glimpse of it
provokes
searing heart pangs
leaving you breathless

This intense sensation
of breaking open
is a seed for you

Turn on the light
move the clutter aside

Reach out
see it
touch it
feel it

Even for a moment
as it
sends forth
the sprout of
your
new
life

Sudden Grace

I feel a sudden grace
a pressing-in
of a thousand unseen faces
touching my eyes
whispering my name
heading towards me
bringing good news
proclaiming their love for me
cradling my cheeks
in their warm
invisible hands
urging me forward
stroking my long hair
handing me the keys
ushering me into
my new beginning
releasing me from the old
midwifing my birthing
of this current
sacred magnificent world

Quench

These my sweet
are the labor pains
of your own soul's birthing

As you ride their piercing waves
wide awake and so tenderly

through the starry hours of the night

Emerging through smoke and rage
and a great churning

your buttery deep knowing
peeks its head above
the stormy sea
of loss and anguish

With eyes peeled of their haziness
and a heart freed
of its sleeping burden

you place your hand
upon the hot shore

bleeding out
the stories
that have caged you

And as you drag
your weary bones
clinking and clanking
over crab shells, driftwood and wet stones
towards the sound of water trickling

with only the taste of your own salty tears
to guide you

to the mossy rocks
encircling
the forest spring

something unexpected
finds you

A caress of presence
with your own body's longing

You drink deeply here
which quenches
at long last

Your trembling and aching need
for enormous
and abiding
earthy love

Enormous Storm

Take me down with you

enormous storm

to the place below the waters

where my body

in stillness

forgets

for a moment

for one...long...deep...breath

that we've only just begun

and that the big work

lies ahead

Not Yet Time to Push

Death is my midwife
as I labor through the bright days
and sweaty nights
She waits between my legs
firmly massaging my wet thighs crooning
"This is going to be a long labor."
With a wild look in Her eyes
She wipes my brow
With a compress made of Rue
Whispering
"It is not yet time to push."

Dream Door

I never saw her face
yet she placed a door in the opening
one she had carved by hand into soft golden wood

The door
the shape of a paisley with deep grooves and cracks
where light slipped through
with swirls and curls unfolding in motion
an angled asymmetrical tale
told by a blade

She slid the door into
the entryway of the small home
made of clay or snow or butternut squash

She made a circle of round cold stones
and lit a fire inside them
with only three logs
of Birch
white bark curling
arranged crisscross
on the
dusty ground
in front of the door
so the lines she sliced into it danced
in the flickering glow
like a changed mind
a new direction
knowing soon
the home would
wash away
or melt
or be eaten
or rot

The door seemed more trustworthy
than where it led
The gentle rain quelled the fire
to fizzle and steam

I ran to get more firewood
to build up the flames
to show that her efforts were not in vain

But the wood was too wet
and of no help
at all

She had gone
so I traced the pathways of the door
with my bare fingertips

And I heard the song
the song of the door
calling me westward
and inward
and down

The door's melody
calling me
to a great motion
in which the doorway itself
is the seed
of my becoming

Skeleton Wolf

Your eyes penetrate me
in my dreams
I see the hair around your ears
move in response
to the wind

You change
into a skeleton wolf
and fall
to the ground

A thousand tiny sprouts
grow up between your bones
and rise into trees
as new fluffy pups are born
and play
in wrestling snarling joy

You show me
even in this time of dying
how the cycles of nature
keep spinning
always turning towards
the birth of spring

Though this winter of struggle is long
and hope is hard to come by
I feel your gentle spirit
coaxing me to follow
as you lead me
into the heart
of the mountain
where the council of animals speak

Put your bare feet
on the earth
and listen
Allow all the chaos
to swirl out and down
Breathe in the essence
of the ground
that holds you
and fills you
with sweetness
We are here with you
loving you in your folly

Return
to the story the old rocks tell
and the song of the mountain spring

Taste the wild herbs
before they flower
and drink their bitter roots in autumn

Remember
there is a deeper pulse
than the human drama unfolding

We are all here watching you,
watching, and waiting

Being Human

A space in my chest exploded
Some sensations are so strong
they can't be suppressed
rip—squeeze—compress
Am I dying?
Will I break?
Breathe....This is being human

Hatch

The chaotic fire
of my being
burns
The dying
structure
of wood
coaxing open
the cache
of stagnant
buried
lies

Awakening
the scattered seeds
of dreams

Through the flames
I see whispers
of
crystal
stone,
bone
and bud

Through the choking smoke
shining beneath the dur and whir
of way too much
all at once

Bare tender winter feet
sink depressions
in the sand
holes fill with sea water
tears drip on waking face

We are not lost
we are finding a deeper truth
We are not broken
we are hatching

Your Silky Waters

Hello deep stillness
I've never met you before

Were you here all along
under the raging landslide
of *How could they have done this to me?*

Have you been just silently
holding a place for me
under the screams and thrashing
of inner shocked and disembodied children?

Dark pool of wellness
have you been resting down there
beneath the wall
I placed between myself and life?

Until I plunged unexpectedly
through the rubble
beyond the unbearable aching stab
and the horrible sounds
to find myself floating
simply being
in your silky waters?

Sanctuary

I know folx who speak about
what really happened
who share
their rage their tears
their long hidden
selves just waking

The truth
pouring out
of their mouths
Is the road
I travel
back to wellness

They name it
they claim it
I name it
I claim it

We receive support
in this cache of sweetness
this pocket of queer comradery

We witness the spoken No's
the lived loving boundaries
the lines drawn
the contrary paths
of opposite actions taken

That break the chain
of oppression that kills us
that carve out a world
with room for belly breaths
earthy chuckles
fluent expression
and dreams

Where lost poems
forgotten songs
delayed paintings
whole streams
of buried inner selfness
are flowing anew

The seeds of life
coming through
rising up
to surprise and delight us
unleashing
fountains of healing

Thank you, friends
for passing through
the fires of torment
to drink here
with all of us
together

Yours Truly

In the ruffling clouds
my mind settles
I can feel life pulsing in my feet

Every needle on the Pine
out my window
is gently shaking
in response to the ocean air

What did I used to do with my life
before I found you?

How did I use to spend my mornings
before you penetrated them with clarity?

You are the fire in my heart
the scent of my own breath

There is a love here
that is expansive and all-abiding
mysteriously delicious

I feel each grain of sand
on the bottom of my feet
and a sweet contact
as if there are hands holding me from within

One warm palm on my heart
and another meeting it
from within my bosom

Ever since I stopped running from you
there is a wholeness in my breathing

At first it was nearly unbearable to face you
to hear the screams and feel the flashing anger
to be in the seemingly bottomless well
of grief and sadness
to embrace your unending desire
and do nothing about it

This dedication of care and presence for you
has made my world so much brighter,
and with nowhere to hide
I feel found in the dearest of ways

A Message for Trans Kids

There are many who come before you
We are shining bright
holding you in our warmth
We are working
to make
the world a place
where you can smile, live and play
and be celebrated

Until then
tend the flame
of who you are
in your wild creative hearts

Find us
and those who walk beside you

Together we will overcome

The world needs your light

"We have been taught to fear the very things
that have the potential to set us free."
Alok Vaid-Menon

Finale

Thank you for drinking in the labors of my soul. I denied this poetry access to the light of day for many years, pushing it down along with the truth of who I am. My body made it clear over the last few years that it would no longer tolerate this snuffing out of creative fire and hiding of my true identity. I am now living my true gender expression and centering my poetic self, allowing these poems to spring out of me on a daily basis. It is my desire that my writing sparks a discovery and an enlivening in kind, for you, dear reader. I would love to hear from you about what my work awakens in your heart and what you birth in your liberation or what you will birth once you are out of the cages society built for you.

Epilogue

May trans, non-binary and gender non-conforming people everywhere be celebrated, and may we all work together to support and protect the most marginalized of identities, Black Trans Women.[1]   May we listen and respond to their incredibly resilient and powerful voices. May we create a world in which everyone feels free to be who they are.

[1]   Unique Woman's Coalition is a powerful support resource for trans people in the Los Angeles area and a wonderful organization to contribute to in support of Black Trans lives thriving! For more information, please see https://www.theuwc.org

Biography

Keath Silva is a trans herbalist, bodyworker, medium and writer, who lives in the Pacific Northwest and Los Angeles, California. He is of Celtic and Germanic heritage and offers gratitude to the Chumash, Gabrieleño, Yakama, Wishram, Nez Perce, Umatilla, Warm Springs, Wayam and many more groups of indigenous people who have tended the lands he dwells on from time out of mind.

Keath was assigned female at birth and lived much of his life being seen as a girl/woman. As is too common, he experienced violation, abuse and disempowering programming while being perceived as female. In the impulse to overcome this oppression, Keath dwelled deeply in the worlds of expressive dance, breathwork, song, midwifery, Goddess worship, herbalism, bodywork and collective women's healing, and he spent many years assisting countless women in reclaiming their power in private healing sessions, workshops and healing ceremonies.

All those years of sistership, embodiment and earthy connection tended the soil for the deeper truth to emerge and brought to light that which Keath had always secretly known within—he felt more male than female. He often felt that he moved between genders and was beyond all genders. Though wonderfully liberating and satisfying, the process of coming out as trans has been painful and wrought with unexpected difficulties. The poems in this book are the sweat and tears of his transition.

Keath has travelled the depths and wide open spaces in his quest to practice compassion for humans of all genders and to create inclusivity and support to genderqueer, gender non-conforming, non-binary and trans people, as well as cis people.

Currently, Keath offers private healing sessions, mentorships and community workshops to people of all genders for personal healing and collective change.

Keath wearing his Trans T-Shirt by
Mars Wright
(www.marswright.com)